INFORMATION TECHNOLOGY, NATIONAL IDENTITY, & SOCIAL COHESION

A Report of the Project on Technology Futures and Global Power, Wealth, and Conflict

Project Director
Anne G.K. Solomon

Author
Sandra Braman

April 2005

About CSIS

The Center for Strategic and International Studies (CSIS) is a nonprofit, bipartisan public policy organization established in 1962 to provide strategic insights and practical policy solutions to decisionmakers concerned with global security. Over the years, it has grown to be one of the largest organizations of its kind, with a staff of some 200 employees, including more than 120 analysts working to address the changing dynamics of international security across the globe.

CSIS is organized around three broad program areas, which together enable it to offer truly integrated insights and solutions to the challenges of global security. First, CSIS addresses the new drivers of global security, with programs on the international financial and economic system, foreign assistance, energy security, technology, biotechnology, demographic change, the HIV/AIDS pandemic, and governance. Second, CSIS also possesses one of America's most comprehensive programs on U.S. and international security, proposing reforms to U.S. defense organization, policy, force structure, and its industrial and technology base and offering solutions to the challenges of proliferation, transnational terrorism, homeland security, and post-conflict reconstruction. Third, CSIS is the only institution of its kind with resident experts on all the world's major populated geographic regions.

CSIS was founded four decades ago by David M. Abshire and Admiral Arleigh Burke. Former U.S. senator Sam Nunn became chairman of the CSIS Board of Trustees in 1999, and since April 2000, John J. Hamre has led CSIS as president and chief executive officer.

Headquartered in downtown Washington, D.C., CSIS is a private, tax-exempt, 501(c) 3 institution. CSIS does not take specific policy positions; accordingly, all views expressed herein should be understood to be solely those of the author(s).

Library of Congress Cataloging-in-Publication Data
Braman, Sandra.
  Information technology, national identity, and social cohesion : a report of the project on technology futures and global power, wealth, and conflict / author, Sandra Braman.
     p. cm.
  ISBN 0-89206-458-7 (alk. paper)
1. Technology—social aspects. 2. Information technology—social aspects. I. Title.

  T14.5.B695 2005
  303.48'33—dc22

                                              2004031111

The CSIS Press
Center for Strategic and International Studies
1800 K Street, N.W., Washington, D.C. 20006
Tel: (202) 887-0200
Fax: (202) 775-3199
E-mail: books@csis.org
Web: www.csis.org/

Contents

Preface

Throughout 2004, at the request of the National Intelligence Council (NIC),[1] the Center for Strategic and International Studies (CSIS) brought together leaders from advanced technology firms, venture capital enterprises, research universities, and government to consider the geopolitical, economic, and social implications of technological advance out to the year 2020. This publication is one of a series that reflect their deliberations.[2]

The purpose of the exercise was to provide the NIC with ideas and insights relevant to NIC 2020, a project designed to provide U.S. policymakers with a view of how world developments could evolve and to identify opportunities and potentially negative developments that might warrant policy action. The challenge for CSIS was to produce for the NIC analyses that would be useful over time in the face of an explosion of scientific and technological knowledge and with great uncertainties in their paths of growth and patterns of interaction with economic, social, and other forces.

CSIS work included a series of workshops, conferences, and commissioned papers that considered frontier research and innovation and related policy challenges: the global ubiquity of powerful, dual-use technologies; the increasing diversity of players in the global advanced technology enterprise that operate beyond the influence of governments or international governing bodies; and the policy dilemma of balancing security-driven imperatives to curtail the availability of dual-use assets with the need of advanced technology enterprise for openness.

Numerous individuals provided advice and assistance throughout the project. Adrianne George, CSIS program coordinator, provided extensive intellectual and administrative assistance. We owe special debt of gratitude to Dr. Charles A. Sanders, CSIS trustee and project chair, and to Frank C, Carlucci, honorary cochair. CSIS would also like to thank Ambassador Robert L. Hutchings, former chairman of the National Intelligence Council, for his encouragement and support.

Anne G.K. Solomon
Project Director

---

[1] The NIC is a center of mid-term and long-term strategic thinking within the U.S. government, reporting to the director of central intelligence and providing the president and senior policymakers with analyses of foreign policy issues.

[2] Sandra Braman, *Information Technology, National Identity, and Social Cohesion* (CSIS, 2005); Anthony J. Cavalieri, *Biotechnology and Agriculture in 2020* (CSIS, 2005); Gerald L. Epstein, *Global Evolution of Dual-Use Biotechnology* (CSIS, 2005); Julie E. Fischer, *Dual-Use Technologies: Inexorable Progress, Inseparable Peril* (CSIS, 2005); David Nagel, *Wireless Sensor Systems and Networks: Technologies, Applications, Implications, and Impacts* (CSIS, 2005); and Anne G.K. Solomon, ed., *Technology Futures and Global Power, Wealth, and Conflict* (CSIS, 2005).

Information Technology, National Identity, and Social Cohesion

Sandra Braman
Professor of Communication
University of Wisconsin–Milwaukee

This report draws upon discussions at a workshop convened by the Center for Strategic and International Studies on September 23, 2004, as part of the "Technology Futures and Global Power, Wealth, and Conflict" project supported by the National Intelligence Council.

Executive Summary

Information technologies of the twenty-first century are qualitatively different from those of the past in ways that affect the ability of the United States to protect national security. These changes are evident both in the overall nature of the global infrastructure and in the ways in which that infrastructure can be used by individuals and groups. Four features of the global infrastructure affect the context within which national security must be protected in 2020: (1) its increasing capacity; (2) the redrawn map of the global network structure, with a growing role expected for Asian communication; (3) infrastructure vulnerabilities, which include its reliance on energy and normative addressing practices, as well as direct attack; and (4) the unfamiliarity of many sources of contemporary and future innovations of importance.

The global information infrastructure becomes "real" in the actual technological capabilities available to individual users. Five features of today's information technologies as they are experienced by the individual user affect the political potential of the uses of these technologies: (1) the unprecedented computing and communication capacity available to individuals and small groups; (2) the use of software to facilitate the development of particular types of social relations; (3) the ability of individuals and small groups to program and adapt new technologies for their own ends; (4) the ability of individuals to produce content for mass distribution; and (5) the common practice of combining various types of media in order to achieve a single political or social purpose.

The technological features of today's information technologies, both as they shape a global information infrastructure and as they are used by individuals and groups, combine to make possible what sociologists describe as new types of social dynamics as well as enhance the relative importance of some modes of action long available, with the concomitant cost that other long-standing ways of operating are now less effective. Evolving social dynamics of political importance for 2020 include the detachment of political community from geopolitical space that takes place via virtual communities; the development of bimodal communities that combine virtual and face to face interactions; and the appearance of forms of citizenship alternative to geopolitical identification—most importantly, cultural citizenship and global citizenship.

Mobility of communication and access to information have political potential in their replacement of geographic colocation as a basis for community with electronic propinquity and their support for social action via diffuse swarms and smart mobs. Mobilization occurs when community formation is combined with the potential for action; new information technologies offer opportunities for political mobilization through the enhanced effectiveness of groups that are both large and small, tightly and loosely coupled, and composed of strong and weak links. These technologies enable cascades of collaborative political action, but small core groups remain important in determining the focus of such activities and the manner in which they are carried out.

The social dynamics enabled by the use of new information technologies can be used to serve traditional and emergent, as well as conservative and progressive, political ends. The combination of political goals and relationships to technological innovation produces a spectrum of types of political activity using new information technologies that must be distinguished from each other because each requires a different type of response from those seeking to protect national security. These include traditional uses of digital technologies to support authority embedded in traditional types of political organizations, nontraditional but increasingly widespread uses of technologies to mobilize communities seeking incremental change in existing governments, experimental and subversive uses of familiar types of social software to undermine the United States and other existing governments through the practices of terrorism, and the use of completely new technologies invented by those involved in political activity for use in pursuit of either incremental or radical political change. The practice of combining different media to achieve a particular effect appears across this political spectrum.

Using current intelligence and surveillance practices, however, analysts are often unaware of information technology–based political mobilization until specific actions that challenge national security take place. Despite the fact that communication through the electronic network leaves informational traces that can be analyzed in a variety of ways, a number of methodological problems must be addressed. These include interactions among technologies, atypical uses of information technologies, the convergence of technological and political innovation, deliberate undetectability, and research implications of the role of trust in online communication.

The most positive extreme of the spectrum of scenarios for 2020 involving information technology, national identity, and social cohesion would involve reestablishment of trust in the authoritative knowledge of the nation-state and, therefore, in decisions made by the U.S. government. The thriving individual and group identities as expressed in virtual worlds would align with those of the nation-state, and the energies mobilized by participation in virtual communities would support achievement of the goals of the U.S. government. At the opposite extreme, social relations could be chaotic, with trust appearing only within intimate small groups. There could be complete disagreement on which information can be trusted and, therefore, a growing reliance on nonrational modes of argument and decisionmaking. Efforts to protect national identity and national security would be only one among many contending forces seeking to exert control in a highly turbulent environment.

Switching points that will affect which of the scenarios along the spectrum identified by these endpoints include the extent to which individuals learn to evaluate Internet-based information sources, mutual transparency between the U.S. government and its citizens is restored, and emerging cultural identities become incorporated into national identities and activities. Current analytical techniques are inadequate for a full understanding of the social dynamics by which these switching points are operating.

The Technologies

Information technologies of the twenty-first century are qualitatively different from those of the past in ways that affect the ability of the United States to protect national security. These changes are evident both in the overall nature of the global infrastructure and in the ways in which that infrastructure can be used by individuals and groups.

The Global Infrastructure

Four features of the global infrastructure affect the context within which national security must be protected in 2020: (1) capacity; (2) global network structure; (3) vulnerabilities; and (4) the source of future innovations of importance.

Capacity

According to the data presented to the CSIS workshop by Timothy Stronge of TeleGeography, a consulting group that documents the growth of the global information infrastructure and the traffic it carries, the capacity of that infrastructure is so vast today that 90 percent of it is unused. The infrastructure is still growing as measured in each dimension of importance: transmission capacity, storage and processing capacity at individual network nodes, and the number of network nodes. This creates a global communication and information-processing capability unprecedented in human history. Overcapacity encourages the development and use of such bandwidth-rich applications as high-speed transfers of scientific data, real-time video imaging, and centralization of software for use over networks rather than placing software on individual machines. Because this wealth of capacity is unprecedented, however, its ultimate political implications are not yet known.

The Global Network Map

The architecture and capacity of the global network have historically been critical factors in international relations both during peacetime and during war.[1] While intercontinental links between North America and Europe will continue to be important in 2020, much of today's global capacity is in areas of the world that have not played a major role in international communications in the past. According to Stronge, the greatest percentage of unused intercontinental network capacity is among Asian countries and between Asian countries and their active partners. The International Telecommunications Union (ITU)[2] reports that Taiwan, Singapore, South Korea, and Hong Kong are already among the countries with the highest levels of Internet and mobile phone use in the world, and China is experiencing among the fastest rates of increase in each of these areas of all countries. (The United States ranks 11th in the world in level of Internet penetration according to these statistics and is far behind many other countries in the speed with which the mobile phone is being taken up.) China is now the leading market in the world for broadband communication—at speeds eight times those available to the average British user—and the Asian region overall now constitutes 32 percent of the worldwide subscriber base.[3] China is already playing an increasingly important role in content production, and its programming industry is beginning to challenge the globally successful film and television industries of India.[4] The desire for global outreach has been expressed by the

---

[1] Daniel Headrick, *The Invisible Weapon: Telecommunications and International Politics, 1851–1945* (New York: Oxford University Press, 1991).

[2] ITU, *World Telecommunication Indicators 2004* (Geneva, Switzerland: ITU, 2004).

[3] "China leads in worldwide DSL market," ITU Strategy and Policy Unit Newslog, http://www.itu.int/osg/spu/newslog/2004/03/09.html; Jo Twist, "China leads world on broadband," *BBC News*, October 5, 2004, http://news.bbc.co.uk/1/hi/technology/3699820.stm.

[4] "China's pioneering tech giants," *BBC News*, May 25, 2004, http://news.bbc.co.uk/1/hi/world/asia-pacific/3744167.stm.

Chinese government,[5] as well as by its corporations.[6] China is also being deliberately used as a test site for experimentation with new technologies such as Internet-based telephony ("voice-over IP," or VOIP).

The development patterns are different in the Middle East, also a region that has not been very active in global communications in the past but which is likely to be so in the future, with significant political implications. According to workshop participant Marwan Kraidy, an expert in Middle Eastern media, many governments in that region have invested heavily in the development of high-speed information infrastructure within their countries, though that infrastructure is currently neither available to a large percentage of their populations nor very well connected with the larger world. Public-sector investment is slowing down, however, because of the belief that private interests in mobile telephony will take up the task.

Workshop participants did not agree on the question of whether or not access to the key functions enabled by the Internet would ever become universally available across the globe. While some pointed to the results of numerous studies that showed enormous returns on investment in telecommunications networks in developing societies, others reported on the many failures of companies that had tried to serve these areas. There was general agreement, however, that the critical issue in terms of the political impact of information technologies, as well as economic development, was crossing the barrier from no connectivity to the global network to having that connectivity. After that barrier is crossed, additional technological capacity or sophistication in available technologies produces change that is only incremental in comparison.

Vulnerabilities

Although the CSIS Workshop did not directly concern itself with information warfare, the question of how, and in what ways, the global network is vulnerable was considered important from the perspective of its implications for national identity and social cohesion. Stronge assured the workshop that the infrastructure is fairly robust in physical terms thanks to redundancy put in place by network engineers. Hans Binnendijk, of the National Defense University, and consultant Jan Lodal, however, emphasized that conditions under times of peace are likely to be different from those under times of war. They pointed out that relatively little of the global network is hardened sufficiently to protect it during times of war. There was particular concern about the vulnerability of satellites, given their current tactical and logistical importance during the course of military operations.

Decentralization of information flows and deliberate redundancy in the network it difficult to prevent any particular messages from being transmitted, but control over the physical backbone does remain the most effective locus of control over

---

[5] Robert Sutter, *China's Future: Implications for US Interests*, a conference report of the National Intelligence Council (Washington, D.C.: National Intelligence Council, September 1999), http://www.cia.gov/nic/confreports_chinafuture.html.
[6] Yuezhi Zhao, "Transnational Capital, the Chinese State, and China's Communication Industries in a Fractured Society," *Javnost—The Public*, vol. 10, no. 4 (2003): 53–74.

information flows. In a recent example of how such control can be used in response to perceived political activity considered unwelcome, several UK servers used by a global independent news organization, IndyMedia—among other clients—were physically seized by the FBI acting on what were reportedly requests of the Italian and Swiss governments, temporarily disrupting the Web-based distribution of a portion of this organization's news reportage.[7]

Workshop participants identified three additional sources of network vulnerability. First, as was explained by Hans Klein during his CSIS workshop presentation, the normative conventions and social support systems for Internet use established by the "domain name" system of locating Internet addresses is itself a source of vulnerability; should it fail, the Internet would become useless for all intents and purposes for most of the world's population because people would not know how to actually send a message so that it was delivered to the intended recipient.[8]

Second, because the global network is electronic, it is dependent on a steady energy supply. Thus the vulnerabilities in the area of energy become communication weaknesses as well. The heavy energy demands of the computing industry and its network use in California were frequently mentioned as contributory to brown-outs in that state in recent years, and energy-based failures of Internet service providers received legal attention as early as 1997. However, Tim Stronge pointed out during the CSIS workshop that most network planners have taken energy vulnerabilities into account by installing high-capacity batteries and on-site generators at mission-critical facilities. Stronge noted that most telecom switching centers remained operational throughout the most significant energy outage in recent years, which covered much of the northeastern United States and Canada.[9]

Third, the dual-use nature of all information technologies presents a basic problem for those who seek to restrict the use of information technologies in order to protect national security: infrastructure that carries information to support fundamental economic and military activity is the same infrastructure that carries communications used to organize terrorist groups and their activities. As has been widely discussed, the Chinese realized during the 1989 demonstrations in Beijing's Tiananmen Square that communications in support of political resistance could not be shut down without simultaneously damaging the economy and operations of the government. According to a recent U.S. Government Accountability Office (GAO) study of networks used by the Department of Homeland Security, four of the networks currently used by federal agencies for

---

[7] "US seizes independent media sites," *BBC News*, October 11, 2004, http://news.bbc.co.uk/1/hi/technology/3732718.stm.

[8] Those with sufficient technical expertise do not need to rely on the domain name system, but knowledge of how to use the Internet otherwise is available only to a small and vanishingly percentage of the population.

[9] As documented in a reporting service focused on legal problems involving the Internet. See Jonathan Rosenoer and Kimberly Smigel, *Cyberlex*, February 1997, http://www.cyberlaw.com/cylx0197.html.

homeland security purposes are shared with the private sector, and a number of homeland security functions are carried out via the Internet.[10] The same communication system that is used in Brazil to support those involved in education for development purposes, it was noted during the workshop, can also be used by drug cartels.

Future Innovations

The technologies that will have the most political importance in 2020 exist today. As Richard Solomon, president of the U.S. Institute of Peace, pointed out during the CSIS workshop, it typically takes about 20 years for an innovation to achieve social impact. Historian James Cortada of IBM further elaborated: while in some cases the technologies that will be of political importance in 2020 exist only in the laboratory, in many other cases these technologies are already in common use. Still, the question of how innovation processes are changing was clearly of keen interest to those in the workshop, and the topic kept emerging during discussion of other matters listed on the agenda.

Cortada's workshop presentation emphasized that many of today's most important information technologies were U.S. products, and these technologies often came into widespread use throughout the population more quickly in the United States than in other countries because the culture is relatively open to new technologies. Overemphasis on this aspect of U.S. national identity, however, can obscure the interdependencies that have been critical to achieving the current level of technological sophistication in the area of information and communication. While it is popular to treat the Internet as a U.S. invention, for example, the basic notion of packet switching that makes its decentralized architecture possible was developed first in the United Kingdom, and the graphically based Web browser that has been key to mass use of the Internet was developed in Switzerland.[11] Workshop participants agreed that U.S. leadership in technological innovation was weakening as R&D in other regions grows in prominence.[12] As was noted in another CSIS workshop, globalization of knowledge is an important biotechnology issue. The historical importance of international collaborations based on a sharing of technical and scientific knowledge is worth highlighting in light of the rising technological leadership of other countries.

---

[10] Government Accountability Office (GAO), *Information Technology: Major Federal Networks that Support Homeland Security Functions*, GAO-04-375 (Washington, D.C.: GAO, September 2004).

[11] Janet Abbate, *Inventing the Internet* (Cambridge, Mass.: MIT Press, 1999).

[12] India and China are currently receiving the most attention in this regard, though innovations from Korea and Japan remain important and other regions of the world not typically considered active sources of innovation—such as Latin America—are gaining strength in the production of the scientific and technical information on which innovation is based. National Science Foundation, "Latin America Shows Rapid Rise in Published Science and Engineering Articles," NSF press release 04-145, October 21, 2004, http://www.nsf.gov/od/lpa/newsroom/pr.cfm?ni=15100000000129. See also Can Huang et al., "Organization, Programme and Structure: An Analysis of the Chinese Innovation Policy Framework," *R&D Management*, vol. 34, no. 4 (September 2004): 367–387.

Writer Clay Shirky reminded the workshop that not all innovations of political importance involve material technologies. Innovations in legal forms and practices (including the types of lawsuits pursued) can also affect the ways in which individuals and political groups operate and the ability of governments to control those activities. Cortada offered a colonial example of an innovation in social structure involving information processing that was critical to the development of the U.S. approach to democracy: the committees of correspondence combined the use of the printing press, handwritten letters, and face-to-face meetings to develop public opinion on political issues and communicate that opinion among communities in such a way that a larger consensus could be achieved.[13] These examples reinforce the insight of sociologists that organizations are information and communication technologies and that information and communication technologies are ways of organizing ourselves socially. Much of the corporate history of the late nineteenth and twentieth centuries involves multiple iterations of the development of ways of organizing people in order to communicate and process information more efficiently, the replacement of those modes of organization with new technologies that fulfill the same functions, and further cycles of innovation in social form.[14] (Indeed, the first "computers" were rooms full of people systematically working through calculations.) As was pointed out by Lodal, these cycles have long been familiar to students of revolution and of military history,[15] and planning today regularly links together changes in organizational structure, technological innovation, and policies—what is referred to within the military establishment as the "system of systems." The same linkages must be kept in mind during the effort to understand political uses of information technologies today and in the coming decades by those who present challenges to national security. A number of interactions between social form and information technologies are mentioned throughout this report.

A final trend in the nature of innovation that is pertinent to analysis of the political implications of information technologies is the ability of individuals or small groups working on their own to develop new technologies of political importance, discussed further below.

---

[13] This and other historical examples of U.S. innovations in information technologies of political importance are explored in more depth in Alfred D. Chandler Jr. and James W. Cortada, eds., *A Nation Transformed by Information: How Information Has Shaped the United States from Colonial Times to the Present* (New York: Oxford University Press, 2003).

[14] The history of these cycles is described in Joanne Yates, *Control through Communication: The Rise of System in American Management* (Baltimore, Md.: Johns Hopkins University Press, 1989). The relationships and homologies between technologies and organizations are examined from a sociological perspective in Charles W. Steinfeld and Janet Fulk, eds., *Organizations and Communication Technology* (Thousand Oaks, Calif.: Sage Publications, 1990) and from an economic perspective in Arthur L. Stinchcombe, *Information and Organizations* (Berkeley: University of California Press, 1990).

[15] Scholarly treatment of the relationships between organizational form and information technologies as they have affected national security in the past can be found in Chris C. Demchak, *Military Organizations, Complex Machines: Modernization in the U.S. Armed Services* (Ithaca, N.Y.: Cornell University Press, 1991) and in Maurice Pearton, *Diplomacy, War, and Technology since 1830* (Lawrence: University of Kansas Press, 1984).

Infrastructure at the Individual Level

The global information infrastructure becomes "real" in the actual technological capabilities available to individual users. Five features of today's information technologies as they are experienced by the individual user affect the political potential of these technologies: (1) capacity; (2) the use of software to facilitate the development of particular types of social relations; (3) the programmability and adaptability of these technologies; (4) the ability of individuals to produce content for mass distribution; and (5) the common practice of combining various types of media in order to achieve a single political or social purpose.

Capacity

The vast increase in capacity at the global level is replicated at the individual level. A comparison commonly used to dramatize the point is that an ordinary personal computer of today has more computing capacity than the computer used by NASA for its first launches to the moon, and several workshop participants emphasized that dramatic increases in both speed and the size of memory will continue to become available in the coming years. This capacity has political importance because it makes it possible for small groups of people to accomplish some of the types of activities that historically could only be accomplished by large organizations because of the level of resources required. Shirky referred to this shift as the "deprofessionalization" of planning. A second way in which this capacity can affect the mobilization of social groups is through P2P file-sharing, discussed in the next subsection.

The Role of Software

Jennifer Preece, an expert in human-computer interaction, highlighted the ways in which the uses of this individual-level capacity depend on available software. In doing so, Preece turned attention to contemporary Internet-based phenomena that illustrate in a concrete and detailed way the interactions among information technologies, communication practices, and social forms discussed above as they appear at the macro-level of analysis.

Different types of software facilitate particular types of relationships among individuals, and between individuals and information sources. For this reason, Preece described software as "social technologies" that facilitate the development of interpersonal networks and, therefore, communities. She offered several examples of social technologies that do this:

- *Bulletin boards* make it possible for individuals to participate asynchronously in a conversation with multiple threads on a topic or topics of shared interest, the archive of which is always available, and/or require readers to go to them in order to receive information.

- *Listservs* use software that supports the immediate simultaneous distribution of contributions to such conversations through e-mail to everyone who has signed up to receive them. Listservs published by organizations that provide topic-specific daily or weekly news are an increasingly important competitor to news from traditional mainstream news organizations.

- *Blogs* (Web logs), on the other hand, are Web-based journals using software that makes it extremely easy to post texts, images, and links to the Web and to comment on them. Blogs make it possible for individuals to share their opinions with the world, and those few who are genuine opinion leaders attract readerships in the many thousands, making them important political forces in their own right. One example of the political effectiveness of this type of software brought up during the CSIS workshop was the speed with which bloggers successfully produced and distributed the evidence that discredited the *CBS News* report of a memo allegedly providing evidence of a failure to perform by President George W. Bush during his years in the military.

- *Instant messaging* software makes it possible for people to remain in literally constant contact through text messages either while on a networked computer or via a mobile phone with texting capability. This is often used for purely social purposes and is extremely popular with young people who communicate while shopping or barhopping, but the same feature is also used to facilitate real-time synchronization of movements by those engaged in political actions.

- *Avatars* are visual representations that can be individually designed by those who participate in 2-D or 3-D "virtual" communities as a means of expressing or experimenting with their identities. Avatars—or their text-based equivalents—can also play a political role when they are used to disguise the actual identity of the individual contributing to a particular conversation or the source of information provided.

- *Peer-to-peer (P2P) file sharing*, which requires high-speed broadband in order to be practicable, is today's "killer application." P2P now accounts for over 60 percent of all traffic in the United States and higher percentages elsewhere in the world.[16] While sharing music and films are the uses of P2P software with which the public is most familiar, the ease with which this software facilitates transmission of large files between individual users is making this type of software attractive for other purposes, including the transmission of information for use by agencies involved in the protection of national security and homeland security.[17]

Several features of software can contribute to the development and maintenance of trust in groups that communicate largely or exclusively online, a matter critical

---

[16] This data comes from CacheLogic, a firm that does research on peer-to-peer networking. "Global Traffic Levels," June 2004, http://www.cachelogic.com/research/slide12.php.

[17] Details of one example of the use of P2P to support law enforcement can be found in Dibya Sarkar, "Oregon City Builds P2P Network," *Federal Computer Week*, February 23, 2004, http://www.fcw.com/geb/articles/2004/0223/web-medford-02-23-04.asp. There is discussion of using this nationally via the Homeland Security Department in order to most easily and cost effectively share criminal justice files among law enforcement agencies.

to the ability of social groups to function effectively and to mobilize for social action. These include supporting a high level of reciprocity, clarity of scope and commonality of purpose among those participating in a conversation, as well as ease of use. Stability in the servers and networks that support the system is particularly important; Preece reported that communities will sacrifice a great deal in speed and sophistication of the technologies on which they rely in exchange for confidence that they will be able to use those technologies 24/7. Trust is built more quickly when software makes it easy for individuals to share their own stories with a group, and communications within even a task-oriented group are most successful when at least one-third of the messages exchanged are empathetic in nature rather than merely transmitting information.

Other uses of software, however, can destroy trust in ways that affect national identity and social cohesion. Sandra Braman's presentation to the CSIS workshop described the ways in which the constitutionally defined symmetry of knowledge between U.S. citizens and their government, long considered essential to the practice of democracy, is being disrupted by the increase in surveillance of individual communications and network-based behaviors combined with a decrease in access to information about the activities of the federal government itself. This combination has damaging effects both on relations between citizens and their government, as well as on efforts to build trust within virtual and face-to-face communities.

Programmability and Adaptability

Software that is designed for a particular use is often turned to other purposes. Even the e-mail function that remains the most important use of the Internet today was an offshoot of the exchange of technical messages among researchers collaborating in the development of DARPANet, the network out of which the Internet evolved.[18] In an example presented by Preece during the workshop, software developed to support a Web site that was intended to expose children to books from other cultures is now being used by adults interested in language learning.

This adaptability of contemporary information technologies is another key characteristic of political importance for the twenty-first century. Today's information and communication technologies are qualitatively different from the industrial technologies that still dominate how we tend to think about the machines we use because digitization has so vastly multiplied the degrees of freedom with which inputs can be transformed into outputs.[19] Information technologies of course combine hardware, the pieces of which must be industrially produced, and the software that defines just which functions the hardware will perform. While purchasing the pieces of which computers are made and combining them into one's own configuration is an increasingly popular "do-

---

[18] Abbate, *Inventing the Internet.*

[19] Sandra Braman, "Informational Meta-technologies and International Relations," in *Information Technologies and Global Politics: The Changing Scope of Power and Governance*, ed. James Rosenau and J.P. Singh (Albany: State University of New York Press, 2002), pp. 91–112.

it-yourself" activity, the more important implication of the combination of hardware and software from the political perspective is programmability. The open-source movement is a dramatic, highly successful, and well-publicized example of innovation that is taking place outside of typical organizational and financing structures.

In the past, certain uses of information technologies could be controlled through a combination of policy and design because of technological limits. The licensing of broadcasters—which limited the ability to mass distribute content electronically to those approved for this activity by the government—was acceptable even though the First Amendment has been interpreted to forbid the licensing of print media, because it was a technological necessity at the time that the communication regulatory system was established. The same argument cannot be made regarding today's digital technologies, nor can the uses to which these technologies are put be limited at the point of manufacture because new, or different, uses can always be developed through programming by individuals and groups acting on their own. While the U.S. government has been experimenting with various approaches to legally prohibiting certain types of information processing since the 1970s,[20] these have not been successful and are not likely to be because there will always be a work-around.

Of course, the ability to adapt information and communication technologies for uses not intended by those who design and market the equipment is not restricted to digital technologies. Although those who brought the videocassette recorder (VCR) to Latin America and Asia assumed doing so would increase the profits of the commercial film industry, this communication technology was quickly and effectively used in a very different way: to present news from perspectives not previously available. In India, for example, the VCR was used to work around government control over official news broadcasts, and in Nicaragua those seeking a change in government used the VCR to record and distribute reports on community developments and political events from their own perspectives.[21] With digital technologies, however, the range of types of innovations possible is much greater than it was with earlier technologies, as are the speed with which new uses of these technologies can appear and the numbers of people who may be involved in developing innovations. Even commercial software provides extraordinary flexibility for individuals who wish to distribute information on their own and for groups wishing to interact in ways not previously possible.

---

[20] The famous *Progressive* case, which involved publication of instructions on how to build a nuclear weapon, was one early example of an effort to legally prohibit certain types of information processing. Because the information on which the magazine article was based was in the public domain, the government retreated to the argument that, even so, it was illegal to process that information. The argument failed in court. *United States v Progressive, Inc.*, 467 F.Supp. 990 (W.D. Wis. 1979), 4 Med. L. Rptr 2377. See also Sandra Braman, "Differential Application of Constitutional Law by Type of Information Processing," presentation to the Telecommunications Policy Research Conference, Arlington, Virginia, September 23–25, 2000.

[21] Gladys D. Ganley and Oscar H. Ganley, *Global Political Fallout: The First Decade of the VCR, 1976–1985* (Cambridge, Mass.: Program on Information Resources Policy, Harvard University, 1987).

Individuals and Small Groups as Content Producers

Limited technological capacity, the enormity of the financial and technical resources required, and with some media, government regulation all combined to place limits on the number of entities that could produce and distribute content to large numbers of people in the past. Even where there is no government regulation, as is the case for print media in many of the most politically influential countries of North America and Western Europe, almost exclusive reliance on government and government-certified institutions as news sources provides an effective means of ensuring that mass media content is supportive of national cohesion.[22]

As Oliver Boyd-Barrett, a media sociologist who has studied the evolution of news agencies, pointed out during the CSIS workshop, from the 1870s until quite recently, news agencies (many of them directly or indirectly linked to the governments of their respective countries) exercised an immense influence in distilling national and international political and economic news and disseminating this to newspapers and other media both locally and worldwide. Daily news media not wealthy enough (i.e., most) to maintain their own networks of national and international correspondents were especially dependent on the news agencies, but even prestige news media were greatly indebted to agencies as sources of breaking international news and of news from parts of the world that the media did not monitor on a routine basis. Decisionmaking structures internal to news agencies, and to the print and broadcast organizations that subscribed to agency services, ensured that gatekeepers vetted information many times before it was ultimately released.

The combination of government regulation, light level of economic, technological, and institutional resources from the social production and dissemination of information, and rigorous organizational gatekeeping, helped ensure that content released to the public met established standards for data presented as scientific, accurate, or true. Though it was far from absolute, major international and many leading national agencies commanded considerable authority. Additionally, their news portfolios helped to define what counted as being of political and economic significance in the realms of the "national" and "international," and in this respect agency portfolios were generally much more comprehensive than those of client newspaper and broadcast media.

Other characteristics of national news agencies highlighted by Boyd-Barrett as contributing to national identity and social cohesion were the formation of journalistic conventions for establishing objectivity in information presented. Just as stability is important for the building of trust in online communities, so stability of national and international news agencies (which together constituted an

---

[22] A synthesis of decades of studies demonstrating this point can be found in Richard V. Ericson, Patricia M. Baranek, and Janet B.L. Chan, *Negotiating Control: A Study of News Sources* (Toronto: University of Toronto Press, 1989). One example of a study of this enduring phenomenon as it is found across nation-states is Mikhail A. Alexseev and W. Lance Bennett, "For Whom the Gates Open: News Reporting and Government Source Patterns in the United States, Great Britain, and Russia, *Political Communication*, vol. 12, no. 4 (1995): 395–412.

organized and dependable *system* of news exchange among themselves, as well as a system of news dissemination to "retail" media) was an important contribution to whatever degree of authoritativeness was enjoyed by the national governments that provided much of the information passed to and relayed by the agencies.

The fact that the Internet has made it possible to work around all of these historical constraints on content production was of deep concern to CSIS workshop participants, with the topic reappearing several times throughout the day. Shirky described the operations of *Wikipedia*, a collaborative Web-based encyclopedia composed of content contributed by volunteers that presents itself as authoritative, though there has been no systematic gatekeeping and reviewing of the information included. Boyd-Barrett discussed the extent to which ease of publication of news from nonmainstream news sources has undermined the position of national news agencies and the mainstream media. Hans Binnendijk emphasized that our ability to generate and distribute information may be outpacing our ability to evaluate it critically. And several individuals mentioned the difficulty of controlling the spread of rumor, misinformation, and deliberate disinformation on the Web.[23]

These shifts in the types of information to which access is easily available have impacts that extend beyond the sociology of knowledge into the domain of politics. Around the world, governmental control over the news can no longer be assumed. This sometimes, though not always, has the result that democratic practices are able to gain in strength, as many argue was the case with the former Soviet Union.[24] At the same time, however, these changes undermine government control over national identity and, if there are wide disagreements within a population regarding which information sources are to be considered credible, damage social cohesion. As Julianne Chesky, an analyst at the National Intelligence Council, pointed out, even shy of actual polarization, the ease with which individuals can restrict their news reading to sources that present only information in a narrow area or from a certain perspective, contributes to the fragmentation of the sense of a shared public conversation that began with cable television's multiplication of broadcast channels. Workshop participants offered examples ranging from the multilingual broadcasting of the Philippines to current cultural divisions within the political discourse of many European countries. Further, as Boyd-Barrett commented during the workshop, it may be that the loss of sense that there is a source of authoritative knowledge may have created an information environment within which citizens increasingly feel powerless to distinguish between information and misinformation or to independently evaluate

---

[23] The idea that rumors presenting themselves as fact on the Web are rife and that Web users are often willing to treat such rumors as fact—often with damaging social and/or political consequences—has been supported by social science research. See, for example, Diane L. Borden and Kerric Harvey, eds., *The Electronic Grapevine: Rumor, Reputation, and Reporting in the New On-line Environment* (Mahwah, N.J.: Erlbaum, 1998); and Pamela Donovan, "Crime Legends in a New Medium: Fact, Fiction, and the Loss of Authority," *Theoretical Criminology*, vol. 6, no. 2 (2002): 189–215.

[24] Everette E. Dennis and Robert W. Snyder, eds., *Media and Democracy* (New Brunswick, N.J.: Transaction, 1998).

relative quality and dependability. Growing awareness that government policy and regulation impacts the diversity of information sources citizens can access has helped stimulate significant public interest in media policy issues.[25]

Combining Media to Achieve a Single Political or Social Purpose

There are two senses in which media can be combined to achieve a political or social purpose: (1) different information technologies can be used together to mobilize people in ways not possible through the use of any single technology on its own; and (2) diverse media content (e.g., news plus entertainment television programming) can be combined to yield a political effect that would not be achieved in response to either type of content on its own. Marwan Kraidy's presentation to the CSIS workshop, based on 10 years of field research in the Middle East including 5 months during the summer of 2004, provided detailed information about how both of these ways of combining media are changing the political environment of the Middle East in ways that will have global consequences.

In one striking example, the combination of entertainment television programming, instant messaging, and the telephone transformed AIDS from a problem that was ignored by the news—and that many governments in the region refused to even admit was an issue—into a matter of high political salience across the region, responsibility for which was acknowledged at the top level of government. This process started when a Lebanese television "social" or entertainment talk show, with a format that includes questions to guests from both the studio and viewing audience, offered individuals with AIDS to tell their personal stories on the air about how difficult it is to get medical treatment, establishing the existence of actual AIDS victims and introducing the political issue of whether or not adequate medical care is being provided. Members of the audience used instant messaging to alert each other to the television show as it was on the air, increasing the program's audience and triggering individuals who were concerned about the issue to place telephone calls to the show while it was still on the air. The minister of health became aware that there were complaints about the level of health care being provided by his department—either because he was watching the show himself or because someone had communicated with him about it by telephone or instant messaging—and called in to offer a defensive response to critiques of his performance as a government official. In the course of doing so, he tried to shift responsibility to the minister of finance who, he claimed, had not provided those in health with sufficient funds to deal with the AIDS problem. At that point the minister of finance, too, called in to defend himself. By the time the television program was over, everyone in the region knew that AIDS is a real problem that requires political attention, and top

---

[25] Milton Mueller, of Syracuse University, is currently conducting research into the growth of this movement at the international level and has already published a report on its growth within the United States. Milton Mueller, *Reinventing Media Activism: Public Interest Advocacy in the Making of U.S. Communication-Information Policy, 1960–2002* (Syracuse, N.Y.: Convergence Center, Syracuse University, 2004).

government officials had publicly admitted that they had the responsibility to deal with this issue. Over the following months, national governments in the Middle East region were forced to respond to this by taking action to deal with AIDS for the first time.

Other examples provided by Kraidy included a strengthening of the women's movement throughout the region among individuals who communicated with each other about images of women presented in television programming and open challenges to religious figures by unveiled women seen on-air, and ways in which public responses to lifestyle choices presented in entertainment television forced a number of other social issues onto the official political agenda.

These examples highlighted three points, each of which is examined in more detail below. First, none of the technologies used on its own could have generated the significant political outcome achieved, but the use of a combination of technologies did, a finding with implications for methods used in analysis. Second, though analysts habitually focus on news and other explicitly political media content, in the Middle East it is entertainment programming that is having the largest political impact. Even in countries where political expression is repressed, populations find that entertainment programming provides, in essence, proxy subjects for public discourse that cannot be stopped. Because this response would not appear in environments in which both news media and citizens are free to explicitly discuss shared issues of public concern without direct or indirect restraints on what is permitted, it is the combination of constrained news programming and political debate with the nature of entertainment programming that makes this political effect possible. Kraidy's presentation focused on the Middle East, but the impact of entertainment television programming on political mobilization experienced as both negative and positive by national governments has also been documented as it was experienced in the United States in the 1960s,[26] in India,[27] and elsewhere.[28] Third, the separation between cultural community and geopolitical territory facilitated by the use of information technologies has political importance; as demonstrated in the Middle East, public discourse about political issues occurs at the regional level, while government efforts to control and inhibit that discourse takes place—less and less effectively—at the national level.

New Information Technologies and Social Dynamics

The technological features of today's information technologies as they shape both a global information infrastructure and as they are used by individuals and groups combine to make possible what sociologists describe as new types of social

---

[26] Aniko Bodroghkozy, "A Gramscian Analysis of Entertainment Television and the Youth Rebellion of the 1960s," *Critical Studies in Mass Communication*, vol. 8, no. 2 (1991): 217–230.
[27] William J. Brown, "Prosocial Effects of Entertainment Television in India," *Asian Journal of Communication*, vol. 1, no. 1 (1990): 113–135.
[28] Michael Gurevitch and Anandam P. Kavoori, "Television Spectacles as Politics," *Communication Monographs*, vol. 59, no. 4 (1992): 415–420.

dynamics as well as enhance the relative importance of some modes of action long available, with the concomitant cost that other long-standing ways of operating are now less effective. These social dynamics can be utilized in diverse combinations for a range of different political purposes, the subject of the next section of this report. There was a consensus among workshop participants, however, that social processes triggered or enabled by the use of information technologies unfold at different speeds in diverse cultures, economic situations, and base level of technological development. Demographics, level of user experience, and motivations for use make a difference at the individual level.

Detachment of Political Community from Geopolitical Space

The process of detaching community from shared physical space began long before the digital era. The telephone made it possible to sustain frequent communications among those involved in personal and community relationships even when the individuals involved were widely dispersed geographically. With the advent of the use of geosynchronous satellites in the early 1960s, simultaneous global television broadcasts became possible and viewing of such events as President John F. Kennedy's funeral and the Muhammad Ali–George Foreman boxing match in what is now the Congo (the famed "Rumble in the Jungle") began to create a shared cultural space across national borders. With the Internet, however, the possibilities for forming and sustaining community life across a diverse range of types of activities—including political mobilization—has been significantly enhanced. In some cases, new types of communities are appearing that are essentially completely virtual in nature even though they influence what happens in the offline world. In other cases, "bimodal" communities involve both electronic and face-to-face communication that find their capacities enriched because of new information technologies. Both of these have an impact on the identity and cohesiveness of the United States and other nations because they encourage and enable the strengthening of political identities oriented around alternatives to geopolitically based citizenship. As this happens, both national identity and social cohesion weaken.

Virtual Communities

While it generally takes longer to develop trust in online communities than it does when social groups are based on face-to-face personal interactions, trust can be achieved through electronic communication that is just as strong as that experienced in geographically based groups. Several features of the social technologies, or social software,[29] described above support interactions among communities that can be as enduring as those that develop face to face. Information technology–based vehicles for community life combine these features in diverse ways.

---

[29] A history of what is currently being referred to as social software, which started in the 1940s, highlighting the evolution of features of political importance, can be found in Christopher Allen, "Tracing the Evolution of Social Software," Life with Alacrity, October 2004, http://www.lifewithalacrity.com/2004/10/tracing_the_evo.html.

- *Community-oriented Web sites* offer various combinations of resources of value to community members, pertinent news, links to related communities, and often, listservs or other means of facilitating communication among group members. Such Web sites typically both support internal community functions and serve as an interface between the community and other social groups, as exemplified by the Web site of the Inuit community of northern Canada.[30]

- *"Usenet" groups*, which use bulletin boards for asynchronous communications among group members, are one of the oldest support systems for online communities. The browser company Google recently bought usenet group archives and currently hosts these groups.[31]

- *Listservs* can be designed specifically to support particular communities.[32] One feature of listserv software that is particularly of value in shaping communal identity is the accessibility, stability, and comprehensiveness of community memory in the form of always-available archives.

- *Personal lists* can be easily formed using common e-mail software such as Eudora or Outlook Express in support of communities that are either ephemeral and task oriented or very personal. Members of extended families, for example, often create lists to make it easy to communicate with everyone in the family at once.

- *Virtual worlds* are software-driven 2-D or 3-D environments that are used by communities in three ways: (1) free or inexpensive software can be used to create a shared visual as well as textual space for communications among group members; (2) individuals can participate in hosted virtual worlds in much the same way as one participates in urban life on moving to a new city; and (3) communities form around participation in the highly structured virtual worlds of electronic games.

- *Virtual enhancement* of local communities, as in the use of holographic overlays of historic Roman sites using affordable and mobile technologies now available to tourists, contribute to the identity of such locales and/or of the countries of which they are a part.

A community has long been understood as a network of interpersonal relations that provides sociability, social support, a sense of solidarity, and social capital (resources that make it possible for individuals to get things done). Communities are strongest when they involve close friendship or kinship relations, interaction is easy and frequent, and there is intimacy in the sense of a shared desire to be together. Additional features, however, have been identified that characterize

---

[30] To see the complete range of communal activities and relationships supported by this Web site in English, go to http://www.tapirisat.ca/english/main.htm.

[31] A complete index of usenet groups and access to those that are open to new members can be found at http://groups.google.com.

[32] There is now competition between software packages used for this purpose though they are now generically referred to as "listservs." An index to all of the listservs that use the original listserv software can be found at http://www.lsoft.com/catalist.html. There are around 330,000 such lists and over 70,000 of them are open to the public.

strong communities in the virtual environment. Most notably, the assumption that geographic space must be shared by members of a community has been replaced with the notion of electronic proximity or "propinquity."[33] As Clay Shirky put it during the CSIS workshop, the social anchor has replaced the geographic grid as a way of identifying where we are in relation to someone. Network analysis, currently so popular as a quantitative approach to examining social relations, focuses precisely on the strength and distance of social anchors, but it cannot discern the actual nature of those relationships or, necessarily, whether they are based on friendliness or conflict.

Norms for participation in specific online communities are generally built from the ground up, even when virtual communities were created to augment communication among members of preexisting offline communities. Awareness of a need for a shared space for public conversation about shared matters of public concern—precisely the need behind the incorporation of information and communication policy principles in the U.S. Constitution and its amendments—is typically a premiere concern. This has political implications, in that the online experience of insisting upon and developing rules for such spaces is providing socialization in political practice, that is having an influence in the offline world, as is happening in China today.[34] Though experimentation with individual identity, whether for purposes of communal growth or criminal deception, is one of the most common practices on the Internet,[35] virtual communities are most successful when the individual identities of participants are authentic and stable.

Interactivity is just as important in sustaining communities as it is in interpersonal relations. And even shy of actually meeting face to face, the offline contexts within which individuals participate in virtual communities can affect the nature of their participation (e.g., are they being observed while communicating with other members of the community, is it safe and easy to access the community, etc.). Jennifer Preece identified factors that drive people away from online communities, including a lack of useful information or meaningful activity, antisocial behavior by participants in the community, and software support systems that are difficult, time consuming, or complex to use. Those who do not actively participate in community life during the first two months of their entry are not likely to remain members.

Bimodal Communities

Groups that regularly engage in face-to-face communication as well as network-mediated communication achieve trust more quickly than those that do not. Even

---

[33] Barry Wellman, ed., *Networks in the Global Village: Life in Contemporary Communities* (Boulder, Colo.: Westview, 1999).

[34] Guobin Yang, "The Co-Evolution of the Internet and Civil Society in China," *Asian Survey*, vol. 43, no. 3 (2003): 405–422; Guobin Yang, "The Internet and Civil Society in China: A Preliminary Assessment," *Journal of Contemporary China*, vol. 12, no. 3 (2003): 453–475.

[35] Experimentation with online identity is one of the most common subjects for social scientists who study the Internet. A comprehensive, provocative, and highly influential introduction to the subject can be found in Sherry Turkle, *Life on the Screen: Identity in the Age of the Internet* (New York: Simon and Schuster, 1997).

those communities that were first created online rather than face-to-face, however, almost always have an unmediated component if they exist for any more than a single ephemeral purpose. Hackers and programmers involved in the global open-source programming community now have annual conferences. Individuals who devote a significant proportion of their resources to participating in global multi-user electronic games—typically viewed as people who live their social lives almost exclusively online—now also deliberately rent in the same apartment buildings so that they can not only share wireless bandwidth but also socialize around their gaming interests. And in Korea, social clubs that include "dating couches" are extremely popular among young people devoted to electronic games.

Conversely, it appears today that almost every group that forms in geographic space to achieve a social or task-oriented purpose now also uses the Internet to support those goals. Several workshop participants contributed anecdotal examples of this type of bimodal community from their personal lives. Thus, while popular and research attention has focused largely on the formation of nonspace-based, often global, virtual communities, today's information technologies can also strengthen groups that are very local. Indeed, the very ability to conduct many forms of business at a distance has reversed the process of urbanization in some regions because individuals can now remain in locations they may prefer for aesthetic or personal reasons. Despite decades of perhaps utopian claims that communicating via the electronic network would replace travel for many purposes, James Cortada and other CSIS workshop participants provided examples of ways in which electronic communication actually stimulates travel precisely because people find that face-to-face interactions significantly strengthen online relationships.

Alternative Forms of Citizenship

The growth of purely virtual and bimodal communities offers a significant challenge to the U.S. and other national governments in the form of the replacement of geopolitical affiliations—citizenship as traditionally conceived—with other types of political affiliations. Three alternative forms of citizenship, each of which draws political energy away from national governments, are growing in strength as a result of the use of new information technologies: (1) cultural citizenship; (2) global citizenship; and (3) "thin" citizenship. The first two of these are clearly encouraged or enabled by the use of today's information technologies. The growing strength of cultural and global citizenship relative to that of geopolitical citizenship is enhanced by the reduction in commitments by national governments to their citizens, described as a thinning of the citizenship relation, that is the combined product of the privatization of formerly public activities, the effort to reduce the size of government, and the growth of regional governments such as the European Commission.[36] It is to these kinds of

---

[36] James A. Caporaso, "Transnational Markets, Thin Citizenship, and Democratic Rights in the European Union: From Cradle to Grave or from Job to Job?" paper presented to the International Studies Association, Los Angeles, California, March 2000.

developments that Bill Anderson, of the National Intelligence Council, was pointing when he asked participants in the CSIS workshop to try to address the question of how the use of today's information technologies might be undermining allegiance to national governments.

Cultural citizenship, in which cultural affiliations become more important than relationships with a national government, is increasingly a driver of political activity, for culture is the "ideological battleground of the modern world-system."[37] The potential capacity of cultural groups dispersed across geopolitical boundaries to act effectively in global politics is not trivial. As Sandra Braman noted during her presentation to the CSIS workshop, the economy of "cultural China"—China, Taiwan, and the diasporic Chinese community—is the third largest economy of the world when mapped against those of nation-states. Because they are novel, media attention often focuses on the new types of communities that are forming in the electronic environment referred to as "cyberspace." However, just as indigenous groups found that the telephone made it possible to sustain many aspects of traditional community life even when members of those groups became dispersed geographically because of labor conditions,[38] so many cultural groups in the United States and other parts of the world are finding that use of the Internet can strengthen their cultural identity. In an example with implications for national identity and social cohesion in the Middle East, a Kurdish media Web site has the declared mission of offering a "united Kurdish voice."[39] One recent story published on this site reported on the motivations of a Kurdish filmmaker who "picked up a camera because I was helpless" and whose goal is "to make this machine speak in Kurdish."[40]

A sense of *global citizenship* is developing among those who are forming virtual communities around issues, such as environmental problems or the situation of women, rather than culture. The use of information technologies is key both to the perception that individuals in many nation-states are a part of a single global civil society and to the ability of those individuals and of nonprofit organizations from many countries to coordinate their activities in pursuit of shared goals. The results of the 1992 "Earth Summit," the UN Conference on Environment and Development in Rio de Janeiro, for example, were unprecedented in large part because this was the first international conference during which nonprofit environmental groups effectively used information

---

[37] Immanuel Wallerstein, "Culture as the Ideological Battleground of the Modern World-System," in *Global Culture: Nationalism, Globalization, and Modernity*, ed. Mike Featherstone (London: Sage Publications, 1990), pp. 31–55.

[38] Heather Hudson, *When Telephones Reach the Village: The Role of Telecommunication in Rural Development* (Westport, Conn.: Greenwood Press, 1984).

[39] See http://www.kurdmedia.com.

[40] Jim Quilty, "Laughing into the Void, Making the Machine Speak Kurdish," *Kurdish Media*, October 21, 2004, http://www.kurdmedia.com/reports.asp?id=2231. (Originally published in the *Daily Star*.)

technologies to draw on data and knowledge from around the world to develop real-time inputs into analysis and decisionmaking on a daily basis.[41]

The first time that civil society had an official presence at the table in discussions of an international organization took place in December 2003, at the International Telecommunications Union (ITU) World Summit on the Information Society (WSIS) meeting in Geneva, a conference devoted to the question of how to best represent the interests of all of the world's peoples in the global governance system developing for the Internet and other technologies of the global information infrastructure.[42] The interaction between the use of information technologies and the emergence of global citizenship is highlighted by the fact that global civil society was first acknowledged as a reality that must be dealt with in international decisionmaking within the context of this particular organization, for the ITU—created in response to the need to transmit telegraph messages across borders and with responsibilities for dealing with information technologies ever since—was the first international organization, has been the most enduring international organization, and is often referred to as the "ideal type" for international regimes.[43]

The regional movements around social issues in the Middle East are examples of a transition stage between geopolitical and other forms of citizenship that offer additional insight into ways in which cultural citizenship and global citizenship can themselves be in tension with each other. In the cases discussed by Kraidy, those who seek political responses to regional and global issues such as AIDS often find themselves in conflict with those for whom the primary identity is as believers in Islam, irrespective of the nation-state in which they find themselves.

Mobility

Wireless and mobile information and communication technologies are disruptive innovations in every sense of the word. Economically, these innovations are undermining long-successful corporations and industries; socially, they are making possible unfamiliar behaviors and effects. It is too early to predict all of the ways in which mobile communication, information access, computing capability, and sensory input will transform the political environment, but it is already clear that new types of social groups are appearing that are capable of the political action—mobilization—that is the subject of the next section of this report. This can be seen in the growing importance of electronic collocation over geographic proximity, diffuse swarms, and smart mobs.

---

[41] Rory O'Brien and Andrew Clement, "The Association for Progressive Communications and the Networking of Global Civil Society: APC at the 1992 Earth Summit," *CPSR Newsletter*, vol. 18, no. 3 (Summer 2000), http://www.cpsr.net/oldsite/externalSiteView/publications/newsletters/issues/2000/Summer2000/obrien-clement.html.

[42] See http://www.itu.int/wsis/.

[43] George A. Codding and Anthony M. Rutkowski, *The International Telecommunication Union in a Changing World* (Dedham, Mass.: Artech House, 1982); Mark A. Zacher and Brent A. Sutton, *Governing Global Networks: International Regimes for Transportation and Communications* (Cambridge: Cambridge University Press, 1996).

Collocation

As discussed above, new information technologies have replaced geographic collocation with electronic propinquity as a basis for community. The same shift influences how people interact for ephemeral social and other purposes, whether or not the groups of people involved ultimately develop a more enduring structure. Of course, as Hans Klein pointed out during the CSIS workshop, even those collectivities that appear to dissolve once a particular task has been accomplished or event has occurred leave enduring traces in the form of social capital; that is, in relationships that have been formed or strengthened, information that has been exchanged, and trust that has been enhanced. Robert Hutchings, chairman of the National Intelligence Council, reinforced the point that all these elements of relationship-based social capital remain available, whether formalized or not, as seeds for future collective action—and the very knowledge that this is so contributes to the ephemerality of specific group formations.

One example of the use of social software for ephemeral organizing purposes, offered by Clay Shirky, called Dodgeball, combines global positioning system (GPS) mapping and communication functions. As often happens with digital technologies, users of Dodgeball change the ways in which they use it once they gain experience. While at first people used this software to answer questions such as "Where is that bar?" in order to make their plans for a social evening, they soon turned to asking "Where are my friends?" as Cartesian mapping functions were replaced by a coordinate system oriented instead around people. Other software is now in use that allows people who do share physical space such as a club to communicate electronically in order to determine whether or not to strike up an actual face-to-face conversation with someone seen across the room. Though these are uses of mobile information technologies to link electronic and geographic collocation for social purposes, the same technologies could be used for political ends.

Diffuse Swarms

Parents have long complained that their teenagers spend too long on the telephone simply chatting with their friends. With cell phones, however, this behavior has become more extreme. Young people may be on their cell phones literally dozens of times between dinner and bedtime, and the sight of individuals in constant conversation on their cell phones while walking down the street or driving is familiar to all. Jennifer Preece described shopping for clothes in Paris with her daughter, who remained on the cell phone the entire time with her boyfriend in the United States discussing whether or not to buy particular items of clothing, which he was also able to see through use of the camera function of the phone. Beyond the anecdotes, or the annoyance, these communicative relationships actually represent a new form of social organization, a diffuse swarm of individuals who are in constant contact irrespective of their physical locations. Again, while diffuse swarms are primarily social in nature, the same functions of information technologies can be turned to other purposes.

Smart Mobs

Smart mobs link collocation with mobilization.[44] A smart mob appears when mobile communication devices have been used to direct geographically dispersed people to gather at a particular location to undertake a specific action. Smart mobs are also often social in nature, with crowds gathering for a single shared play event such as descending on a furniture store so that everyone in the crowd can try out one sofa or showing up at a book store to ask about books that don't exist. According to one individual interviewed for a BBC news story, it is precisely the point of this type of smart mob—also known as a flash mob—that there is no ideological content or goal at all.[45]

Smart mobs are also becoming characteristic of political demonstrations, however. Shirky used the well-known example of the "Battle for Seattle" demonstrations against a meeting of the World Trade Organization (WTO) in that city in 1999 as a focus for his comments on this phenomenon, noting the flexibility of movement during the course of an event that this approach to political organizing made possible. Smart mobs have since been used in antiglobalization demonstrations in other cities around the world as well as in demonstrations during the Republican National Convention in New York in 2004. Some would even extend the concept of smart mobs to groups that convene for political purposes after being alerted to do so via a Web site that operates in much the same way as posters on telephone poles were used to convene protesters during earlier periods.[46]

It must be emphasized, however, that the political potential of smart mobs, the appearance of politically effective smart mobs, and the reality of the politically oriented smart mobs that have so far been experienced are three different things. Conceptually, there is the potential that mobile communications devices— particularly when combined with access to detailed information such as that offered by global positioning systems and databases—could make it possible for groups to convene essentially spontaneously and engage in politically effective activities. For the media, and in popular perception, the appearance that this is currently being done has been persuasive. In reality, a great deal of prior planning has gone into preparing the large demonstrations, such as the seminal event in Seattle, with groups being trained in how to communicate quickly, briefly, and effectively as well as how to act once they arrived in certain locations.

Though it was suggested during the CSIS workshop that these technologies make it possible to replace planning before activities take place with real-time coordination of events while they take place, prior planning has not disappeared but, rather, has a different substantive focus. Instead of training people in specific

---

[44] The term "smart mob" was coined by Howard Rheingold, who has been involved in electronic communities since the first enduring group, known as The Well, several decades ago. Howard Rheingold, *Smart Mobs: The Next Social Revolution* (New York: Basic Books, 2003).

[45] "Smart Mob Swarms London," *BBC News*, August 8, 2003, http://news.bbc.co.uk/1/hi/technology/3134559.stm.

[46] Chris Taylor, "Day of the Smart Mobs," *CNN.com*, March 3, 2003, http://www.cnn.com/2003/ALLPOLITICS/03/03/timep.smart.mobs.tm/.

tactical moves regarding where to be when, preparation is directed at the logistical questions of how to design and carry out tactics in the field. This is still a qualitative change in how political engagements are carried out, but appreciation of the full range of pertinent processes involved requires going beyond the simple and dramatic discussions of these developments that currently dominate public perception.

Mobilization

While mobility was an obvious candidate for CSIS workshop discussion, it was Mark Levy, a professor of communication who was among the first in that field to take seriously the political implications of new information technologies, who pointed out during the CSIS workshop that mobility and mobilization are two different things. He argued that mobilization should really be added as a third term to the subject of this study since neither national identity nor social cohesion really matters if action is not enabled. Klein linked together various strands of workshop discussion in his comment that social action always depends on the ability of dispersed individuals to act or work together as a community or organization, and it is this type of collective action that is the building block of politics. The potential of new information technologies to effectively mobilize political action can be seen in their impact on group effectiveness and collaborative political action. Small core groups remain important for mobilization in the information environment of the twenty-first century.

Group Effectiveness

While Preece's presentation to the CSIS workshop identified specific features of software that make particular types of collective action possible, Shirky's focused on the impact on group effectiveness once such software comes into use.

As context for the detail offered, he highlighted the fact that it is an error to assume that once one type of effect of the use of information technologies is observed that there are not other, even opposite, effects. This notion is familiar from the 1960s work of Marshall McLuhan, who is most famous for his prediction that new information technologies would break down national barriers and create a "global village," and his insights into the way that the medium through which information is received shapes both the ways in which we process that information and which of our senses dominates how we relate to the material and social worlds around us ("the medium is the message"). McLuhan claimed that we should expect to find simultaneous but opposite effects of the use of information technologies, even when used in the same ways in the same context.[47]

---

[47] Marshall McLuhan's ideas as presented in numerous books during his lifetime were synthesized after his death into a single comprehensive framework in Marshall McLuhan and Eric McLuhan, *Laws of Media: The New Science* (Toronto: University of Toronto Press, 1988). Though McLuhan largely chose to present his ideas in forms that would appeal to a wide public audience rather than to scholars, appreciation of the accuracy and the importance of his insights has grown over time, and over the last decade growing numbers of researchers have translated them into forms that can be studied systematically. This work is considered so important today that it has spawned a new

The history of the impact of the introduction of the printing press and movable type into Western civilization from 1450 on provides abundant evidence that this is a characteristic of all information technologies, not just those of the digital era.[48] In a pertinent and significant precedent for what might be expected of the nature and locus of political power in the twenty-first century as a result of the use of new information technologies, the printing press both strengthened the ability of the incumbent institution of the Catholic Church to exert control and stimulated the development of Protestantism and the shift of power to secular entities that ultimately evolved into the modern nation-state.

The same duality can be seen in the consequences of the use of mobile and digital technologies for the ability of groups to engage in political action, whether large or small and whether composed of relationships that are weakly and/or loosely coupled as opposed to those in which they are strongly and/or tightly coupled.[49] While small groups can be more effective in what they do, it is also true that larger groups can more easily be coordinated than they were in the past. Tightly organized groups can hide better, while loose groups can form and dissolve faster. Highly committed cores can get better leverage in large groups, while groups of those previously uncommitted can also get more done. Highly centralized organizations such as those of national governments can exert control at a finer level of detail and over a greater scale, but decentralized groups can also achieve coordinated action. The transparency that is made possible by the nature of the global information infrastructure links the global with the personal and local in ways that also affect the nature of mobilization in today's environment.

Collaborative Political Action

Bill Anderson described the contemporary situation as one in which information technology–enabled political action is taking place among groups largely acting on their own, and he drew CSIS workshop attention to the question of what the political effects might be when such groups come together for collaborative political action. One engine for such collaborations—for example, the mass demonstrations in Leipzig in 1989–1991—has been described as "informational cascades,"[50] a concept introduced into workshop discussion as "collaborative cascades" by Shirky. One of the features of such cascades is that the interactions involved are nonlinear in nature and thus require political analysis that

professional association among researchers (the Media Ecology Association) and its own journal (*McLuhan Studies*, published by the University of Toronto Press) as well as forming the foundation of work presented in other venues.

[48] See, for example, Elisabeth Eisenstein, *The Printing Press as an Agent of Change: Communications and Cultural Transformations in Early-Modern Europe* (Cambridge: Cambridge University Press, 1979).

[49] Strength and flexibility of coupling are two different dimensions of relationships within interpersonal networks. Strength refers to how powerful and enduring the relationships are, while the degree to which a relationship is loose or tight refers to the degrees of freedom with which interactions may take place within that relationship. David Knoke and Mark Granovetter, eds., *Political Networks: The Structural Perspective* (New York: Cambridge University Press, 1990).

[50] Suzanne Lohmann, "Dynamics of Informational Cascades: The Monday Demonstrations in Leipzig, East Germany, 1989–1991," *World Politics*, vol. 47 (1994): 42–101.

incorporates the insights of complex adaptive systems, or chaos, theory.[51] Another is that they result from interactions among several different types of events. In the case of Leipzig, the informational cascades involved the combination of legalization of opposition political groups, media reportage on environmental and other problems that had not previously been the subject of public discussion, and the opening of the borders, all amplified in the course of public demonstrations. In the case of Seattle in 1999, the cascades derived from more micro-level interactions among the experiences of small groups in isolated parts of the city as communicated to others using mobile technologies.

A third feature of informational cascades that is important for evaluating their likelihood and predicted impact is that they are initially triggered by those who take extreme political positions and whose thresholds for action are relatively low. The kind of large-scale collaboration among groups that yields cascades depends to some extent on the distribution of thresholds to action throughout a population; one reason the interactions are nonlinear is that these thresholds change as the informational and political climates become transformed. Oliver Boyd-Barrett therefore linked such informational cascades to the declining authoritativeness of the media organizations that have supported strong national identities in the past, and he pointed out that entirely new communication campaign tactics and strategies must be developed in order to preempt and/or respond to such processes.

The Impact of Small Core Groups

A final characteristic of informational cascades worth noting is that they are usually triggered by a small group of individuals who have strong incentives for generating collective action. The relative importance of small groups in generating political activity[52] through the use of information technologies was a recurring theme throughout the workshop discussion. Lodal pointed out that even the seemingly democratic developments within the open-source programming community are largely the result of efforts by one to four people. As Cortada put it when elaborating on successful episodes of management change within IBM driven by the formation of *ad hoc* groups utilizing networked communication technologies, even though such change was bottom up in a sense, leadership still counts. And Klein noted that those who fill such roles are most likely to be those who have already mastered the technical skills required to maximize the effectiveness of their use of information technologies. Among the national security implications of this fact, as Binnendijk stressed, is that it may be possible for a minority to have disproportionate influence within a society, even if those involved come from outside of the country; radical Islam was offered as an example of where this might currently be the case.

---

[51] Diana Richards, *Political Complexity: Nonlinear Models of Politics* (Ann Arbor: University of Michigan Press, 2000).
[52] Art Kleiner, *Who Really Matters: The Core Group Theory of Power, Privilege, and Success* (New York: Doubleday, 2003).

Analysis of Political Uses of Information Technologies: The Problems

Knowledge of the nature of the global information infrastructure, of the technologies available at the individual level, and of the social dynamics made possible by the interactions of the two provide a background against which it is possible to see the diverse types of political activity to which these technologies contribute. The social dynamics enabled by the use of new information technologies can be used to traditional and emergent, conservative and progressive, political ends. The combination of political goal and relationship to technological innovation produces a spectrum of types of political activity using new information technologies that must be distinguished from each other, because each requires a different type of response from those seeking to protect national security. These include:

- Traditional uses of digital technologies, such as Web sites and e-mail, can support authority embedded in traditional types of organizations, such as those of Islamic mullahs.

- Nontraditional but increasingly widespread uses of technologies, such as blogs, listservs, and virtual worlds, are being turned to the purposes of developing and mobilizing communities that seek changes in existing governments and legal systems, as in the information commons movement or those who are concerned about some of the effects of trading practices carried out via agreements of the World Trade Organization.

- Experimental and subversive uses of familiar types of social software, such as the one-time use of e-mail addresses and embedding of messages in Web sites devoted to the purpose of undermining the U.S. and other existing governments through the practices of terrorism.

- The use of completely new technologies invented by those involved in political activity through programming and other engineering approaches; these technologies are used both by those who seek incremental change within existing government systems as well as by those pursuing more radical change in those governments themselves.

- The practice of combining different media to achieve a particular effect appears across the political spectrum.

As Anderson pointed out during the CSIS workshop, however, using current intelligence and surveillance practices analysts are often unaware of information technology–based political mobilization until specific actions that challenge national security take place. Despite the fact that, as Shirky emphasized, communication through the electronic network leaves informational traces that can be analyzed in a variety of ways, a number of methodological problems must be addressed in order to solve this problem. These include interactions among technologies, atypical uses of information technologies, the convergence of technological and political innovation, deliberate undetectability, and research implications of the role of trust in online communication.

Interactions among Technologies

The CSIS workshop included discussion of a number of instances in which the most important political effects resulted from interactions among the use of a variety of technologies rather than from the use of a single technology on its own. From the colonial committees of correspondence mentioned by Cortada, to the combination of GPS mapping systems with voice communication and texting capabilities described by Shirky, to the role of instant messaging and the telephone in creating the political effect of entertainment television in the Middle East explained by Kraidy, it is clear that an accurate political reading can only be achieved by looking at suites of technologies as they are actually combined into personal and group technological systems.

The tradition of research on the effects of the use of information technologies, however, has almost exclusively been technology specific, and there is almost no work at all that links together the effects of a technology in one political area or as it shaped one specific activity with those of others also involved in the same area or activity. To cope with these problems, analyses must themselves be conducted in suites, perhaps most effectively through the use of tight collaborations among researchers who each undertake studies designed in such a way that their results can be clearly correlated with what is learned from other studies with the same political focus.

This problem is exacerbated by the fact that the focus on digital and electronic technologies such as the telephone and the Internet has taken attention away from the role of oral communication in face-to-face meetings. As reported by the press, it is believed that Osama bin Laden's location has been difficult to identify because much of the communication surrounding his activities never appears in the electronic networks that are the subject of surveillance. Rather, messages are being carried on foot and transmitted in direct conversations that are not discernible irrespective of the sophistication of network tracking software and algorithms being used.

Communication researchers have been aware that understanding oral transmission is key to analysis of the effects of the mass media ever since the 1930s, when the "two-step flow" was discovered—the fact that most people make sense out of mass media messages not from their own reception of the information but as that information is interpreted orally by opinion leaders in their daily lives. More recently, those involved in designing communication campaigns in developing regions to encourage such things as better health practices have come to realize that traditional oral forms such as storytelling and festivals should be incorporated into campaign design. There has to date, however, been almost no research on the role of oral transmission in chains of communication that work in tandem with electronic media to sustain organizational operations. Further, as Richard Solomon commented during the CSIS workshop, the need to take into account interactions among the effects of different technologies raises the problem to second and third orders of complexity, making prediction even more difficult.

Atypical Uses of Information Technologies

Research on the effects of information technologies focuses on typical uses, but political activity often most effectively occurs through nontypical uses. Researchers are creatures of habit and often repeat or mimic long-standing research questions and approaches even when doing so directs attention away from the problems of deepest concern. The overweening bulk of research being conducted on the political uses of information technologies focuses on the most traditional types of venues and activities, such as news as distributed via the Web sites of familiar types of print and broadcast news organizations[53] and official Web sites of political candidates.[54] This is problematic even for understanding political communication within mainstream U.S. society, for a growing number of people (including a high proportion of the most influential decisionmakers) depend on subject-specific listservs and news aggregators for their news rather than on traditional journalistic Web sites. In another important example, as early as 2000 campaign strategists were using software-driven "bots" pretending to be humans to present comments about candidates in Web-based conversations of all kinds, with political effect likely to have been much greater than that of candidates' Web sites because such input was perceived to be thoughts genuinely offered by fellow citizens.[55]

Convergence of Technological and Political Innovation

There are three ways in which the combination of technological innovation with inventiveness in the design and implementation of political tactics and strategies makes it difficult to identify such activities before the new approaches they make possible are put into use. First, because political activity and technological innovation often appeal to the same individuals, and innovation can effectively be undertaken at the individual or small group level, much effective action is being undertaken by either inventors themselves or by early adopters of new technologies. We know very little about these because of their innovativeness, intentional undetectability, and the lag between the development of new behaviors and research methods capable of identifying and interpreting them. Thus it is difficult for national governments to be aware of technologies that are actually in use by those who will deploy them destructively.

Second, because information technologies are instruments of culture as well as of materials, innovations in cultural habits such as language use, inevitably and additionally confound the ability to consistently track communications and behaviors by disruptive groups irrespective of how much effort is put into

---

[53] For example, an influential series of studies of such Web sites has been conducted over the last few years by the Poynter Institute; results of these studies and discussion of their implications for the practice and analysis of journalism can be found on that organization's Web site at http://www.poynter.org.

[54] Bruce Bimber and Richard Davis, *Campaigning Online: The Internet in U.S. Elections* (New York: Oxford University Press, 2003).

[55] Philip Howard, "Privatizing the Citizen" (unpublished doctoral dissertation, DAI-A 63/11, May 2003).

surveillance by national governments. The use of "Aesopian language," the metaphorical use of language intended to protect politically unwelcome perspectives, is ancient. Cultural and linguistic creativity will always outpace the ability to identify and quantify the effects of that creativity by those seeking to control it.

Third, the very effort to surveil and control uses of information technologies considered unfriendly to a government in themselves trigger further innovation. Research by the Berkman Center for the Internet and Society at Harvard Law School, for example, has discovered a number of technological work-arounds invented by individuals within China seeking access to Internet content censored by their government.[56] Encryption is another area in which there are essentially innovation wars between those who are seeking to break messages encrypted by those unfriendly to the U.S. and other governments and those who develop new approaches to encryption in order to maintain secrecy for their communications.

Deliberate Undetectability

Research focuses on what is visible, but much political activity involving information technologies is designed to be invisible. The problem is exacerbated when the political groups being studied are terrorists seeking to evade public attention altogether. One recent report detailed ways in which, it is suspected, Al Qaeda is able to hide its Web-based communications: using specific cyber cafés and/or computers only briefly, using an e-mail address once and then abandoning it, encryption of messages that appear to be taking part in ordinary ongoing conversation on messages boards, constantly changing the locations of pertinent Web sites, embedding terrorism-related Web sites within sites devoted to other purposes, and possibly, steganography.[57]

During the workshop, Jon Alterman, director of the CSIS Middle East Studies Program, described similar tactics on the part of the Egyptian gay community who would post meeting locations on ephemeral Web sites, encrypt discussion groups, and so forth, in order to try to protect themselves from observation. These are all unfamiliar problems to those who study political communication, and the research tools to cope with such practices are still under development. In the case presented by Alterman, such techniques were taken up after more open communication led to mass arrests of those accused of being engaged in sexual practices considered illegal in Egyptian society, drawing attention again to the importance of trust in online communications.

Research and Trust

The research techniques most used to study digital information flows are quantitative in measure, evaluating the extent to which messages are exchanged

---

[56] Jonathan Zittrain, "Internet Points of Control," in *The Emergent Global Information Policy Regime*, ed. Sandra Braman (New York: Palgrave Macmillan, 2004), pp. 203–227.
[57] Gordon Corera, "A web wise terror network," *BBC News*, http://news.bbc.co.uk/1/hi/world/3716908.stm.

among particular parties, the interpersonal networks suggested by communication flows, and the presence or absence of certain words in messages that are sent. Several workshop participants, however, noted that the heavily used techniques of network analysis, for example, may reveal who is talking to whom but can't really determine just what it is that is being said or the meaning of what is communicated. In an example provided by Anne Solomon, senior adviser for technology policy at CSIS, the frequency of telephone calls between the Middle East and India could be interpreted as suggestive of planning activities among terrorist groups or, more likely, could simply be an function of the number of Indian guest workers in the Middle East who wish to remain in voice contact with their families.

To understand the political effects of nontypical uses of familiar technologies, become aware of innovations developed specifically for political purposes, and learn to recognize what is undetectable, analysts must cross the bridge from quantitative to qualitative techniques. The difficulty of doing so is not merely intellectual, for trust must be achieved before one can gain access to the groups being studied. It took the time-intensive participation of an ethnographic researcher involved with a campaign consulting group, for example, to learn about such political uses of information technologies as the planting of campaign messages via software-driven bots in online conversations as described above.[58] Some of the methodological issues confronting analysts studying the political uses of information technologies can be resolved, but the problem of trust will remain a barrier to acquiring many of the most important forms of knowledge.

Switching Points for 2020

The most positive extreme of the spectrum of scenarios for 2020 involving information technology, national identity, and social cohesion would involve reestablishment of trust in the authoritative knowledge of the nation-state and, therefore, in the decisions made by government. The thriving individual and group identities as expressed in virtual worlds would align with those of the nation-state, and the energies mobilized by participation in virtual communities would support achievement of the goals of the government. At the opposite extreme, social relations could be chaotic, with trust appearing only within intimate small groups. There could be complete disagreement on which information can be trusted and, therefore, a growing reliance on nonrational modes of argument and decisionmaking. Efforts to protect national identity and national security would be only one among many contending forces seeking to exert control in a highly turbulent environment.

Switching points along the spectrum identified by these endpoints include: the extent to which individuals learn to evaluate Internet-based information sources; the extent to which mutual transparency between the U.S. government and its citizens is restored; and the extent to which emerging cultural identities become incorporated into national identities and activities. Current analytical techniques

---

[58] Howard, "Privatizing the Citizen."

are inadequate for a full understanding of the social dynamics by which these switching points are operating.

Appendix: Workshop Participants

Information and Communication Technologies: Social Cohesion and National Identity
September 23, 2004

Peter Ackerman
Founding Chair
International Center on Nonviolent
Conflict

Jon Alterman
Director, Middle East Program
CSIS

Oliver Boyd-Barrett
Professor of Communication
California State Polytechnic
University–Pomona

Hans A. Binnendijk
Director, Center for Technology and
National Security
National Defense University

Sandra Braman
Professor of Communication
University of Wisconsin–Milwaukee

James W. Cortada
IBM Institute for Business Value

Patrick Cronin
Senior Vice President & Director of
Studies
CSIS

Richard L. Engel
Senior Military Analyst
Strategic Assessments Group

Michael L. Haley
Executive Director
International Communication
Association

Hans Klein
Associate Professor of Public Policy
Georgia Institute of Technology

Marwan M. Kraidy
Associate Professor of
Communication
American University

Mark R. Levy
Professor of Telecommunications,
Information Studies, and Media
Michigan State University

James Lewis
Director, Technology and Public
Policy Program
CSIS

Herbert Lin
Senior Scientist, Computer Science
and Telecommunications Board
The National Academies

Jan Lodal
Lodal & Company

Alan Mauldin
Senior Analyst, TeleGeography
PriMetrica, Inc.

Chris O'Brien
TeleGeography
PriMetrica, Inc.

Jennifer J. Preece
Professor of Information Systems
University of Maryland–Baltimore

Teresita Schaffer
Director, South Asia Program
CSIS

Clay Shirky
Writer & Consultant

J.P. Singh
Assistant Professor of
Communication
Georgetown University

Anne G.K. Solomon
Senior Adviser, Technology Policy
CSIS

Richard H. Solomon
President
U.S. Institute of Peace

Tim Stronge
Vice President, TeleGeography
PriMetrica, Inc.

About the Author

Sandra Braman has been studying the macro-level effects of the use of new information technologies and their policy implications since the mid-1980s. Her publications include *Change of State: An Introduction to Information Policy* (MIT Press, forthcoming), *The Metatechnologies of Information: Biotechnology and Communication* (edited) (Erlbaum, 2004), *The Emergent Global Information Policy Regime* (edited) (Palgrave Macmillan, 2004), *Communication Researchers and Policy-making* (edited) (MIT Press, 2003), and *Globalization, Communication, and Transnational Civil Society* (coedited) (Hampton Press, 1996), as well as over four dozen journal articles and book chapters. Dr. Braman served as book review editor of the *Journal of Communication*; is former chair of the Communication Law and Policy Division of the International Communication Association; and sits on the editorial boards of nine scholarly journals. Currently a professor of communication at the University of Wisconsin at Milwaukee, she previously served as Reese Phifer Professor at the University of Alabama, research assistant professor at the University of Illinois at Urbana, Henry Rutgers Research Fellow at Rutgers University, and Silha Fellow in Media Law and Ethics at the University of Minnesota. She earned her Ph.D. from the University of Minnesota in 1988.